Lerner SPORTS

I0886544

WOMEN GOT GAME

WOMEN'S PROFESSIONAL SOCCER

MARGARET J. GOLDSTEIN

Lerner Publications ◆ Minneapolis

Statistics in this book are accurate through August 2024.

Copyright © 2026 by Lerner Publishing Group, Inc.

All rights reserved. International copyright secured. No part of this book may be reproduced, stored in a retrieval system, or transmitted in any form or by any means—electronic, mechanical, photocopying, recording, or otherwise—without the prior written permission of Lerner Publishing Group, Inc., except for the inclusion of brief quotations in an acknowledged review.

Lerner Publications Company
An imprint of Lerner Publishing Group, Inc.
241 First Avenue North
Minneapolis, MN 55401 USA

For reading levels and more information, look up this title at www.lernerbooks.com.

Main body text set in Aptifer Slab LT Pro.
Typeface provided by Linotype AG.

Editor: Evan Villas **Designer:** Mary Ross
Lerner team: Martha Kranes, Sue Marquis

Library of Congress Cataloging-in-Publication Data

Names: Goldstein, Margaret J., author.
Title: Women's professional soccer / Margaret J. Goldstein.
Description: Minneapolis, MN : Lerner Publications, [2026] | Series: Women got game (Lerner sports) | Includes bibliographical references and index. | Audience: Ages 7–11 | Audience: Grades 2–3 | Summary: "Since it began in 2012, the National Women's Soccer League has been full of amazing moments. Explore the league's growth and learn about its best players, such as Lynn Williams, Trinity Rodman, and Naomi Girma"— Provided by publisher.
Identifiers: LCCN 2024038470 (print) | LCCN 2024038471 (ebook) | ISBN 9798765668870 (library binding) | ISBN 9798765683637 (paperback) | ISBN 9798765682258 (epub)
Subjects: LCSH: National Women's Soccer League—Juvenile literature. | Women soccer players—Juvenile literature. | Soccer players—Juvenile literature. | Soccer—History—Juvenile literature.
Classification: LCC GV944.5 .G65 2026 (print) | LCC GV944.5 (ebook) | DDC 796.334/62082—dc23/eng/20240826

LC record available at https://lccn.loc.gov/2024038470
LC ebook record available at https://lccn.loc.gov/2024038471

Manufactured in the United States of America
1-1011983-53858-12/10/2024

TABLE OF CONTENTS

EYES ON THE BALL

The Gotham Football Club was on the move. Jenna Nighswonger fired the ball across the field to Esther González. González passed it to Lynn Williams. *Bam!* Williams knocked the ball into the goal with her head. With that header, Gotham took a 1–0 lead over the Chicago Red Stars.

It was Williams's 79th career goal. That was a new National Women's Soccer League (NWSL) record. On this day in May 2024, Williams took her place in NWSL history.

The NWSL was formed in 2012. Play began in 2013. Since then, the league has seen thrilling goals, dramatic saves, and come-from-behind victories. Its players are some of the world's most talented athletes. This is their story.

FAST FACTS

- CPKC STADIUM, HOME OF THE KANSAS CITY CURRENT, IS THE FIRST STADIUM EVER BUILT FOR A WOMEN'S PROFESSIONAL SPORTS TEAM.
- A TEAM FROM BOSTON, MASSACHUSETTS, WILL JOIN THE NWSL IN 2026.
- TRINITY RODMAN WAS NAMED ROOKIE OF THE YEAR IN 2021 AFTER SCORING SEVEN GOALS FOR THE WASHINGTON SPIRIT.
- NAOMI GIRMA WAS NAMED DEFENDER OF THE YEAR IN 2022 AND 2023.

Chapter 1

A LEAGUE OF THEIR OWN

The US Women's National Team celebrates winning the 1999 World Cup.

In 1999, the US Women's National Team won the World Cup. Americans everywhere were excited about women's soccer. But the United States didn't have a professional women's soccer league.

A group of players, businesses, and sports groups decided to start one. They formed the Women's United Soccer Association in 2000. It operated for three seasons but ran out of money. The league had to shut down.

Soccer lovers tried again. They organized Women's Professional Soccer. This league had money trouble too. It closed after three seasons.

Michelle Akers shoots the ball during a 1999 match against China.

Fans still wanted a women's professional league. A group created the NWSL in 2012. This league prospered. The NWSL made deals to show games online and on TV so more fans could watch. Big companies signed on as sponsors.

Meanwhile, soccer grew more popular in the US. Many kids played the sport and wanted to watch it on TV. They wanted to watch games in person at stadiums. Many NWSL players were already world famous. They had played at the World Cup and the Olympics. Fans tuned in to NWSL games to see these star players in action.

Around three million kids play soccer in the US.

MID-CENTURY ROOTS

The first US women's soccer league formed in 1950 in St. Louis, Missouri. The Craig Club Girls Soccer League had four teams: the Bobby Soccers, the Coeds, the Flyers, and the Bombers. About 70 young women played in the league. It ran for two years.

Two teams from England play a soccer match for a large crowd in 1954.

FIRST OF ITS KIND

CPKC Stadium (*below*) opened in Kansas City, Missouri, in 2024. It is the home of the Kansas City Current. It is the first stadium ever built for a women's professional sports team.

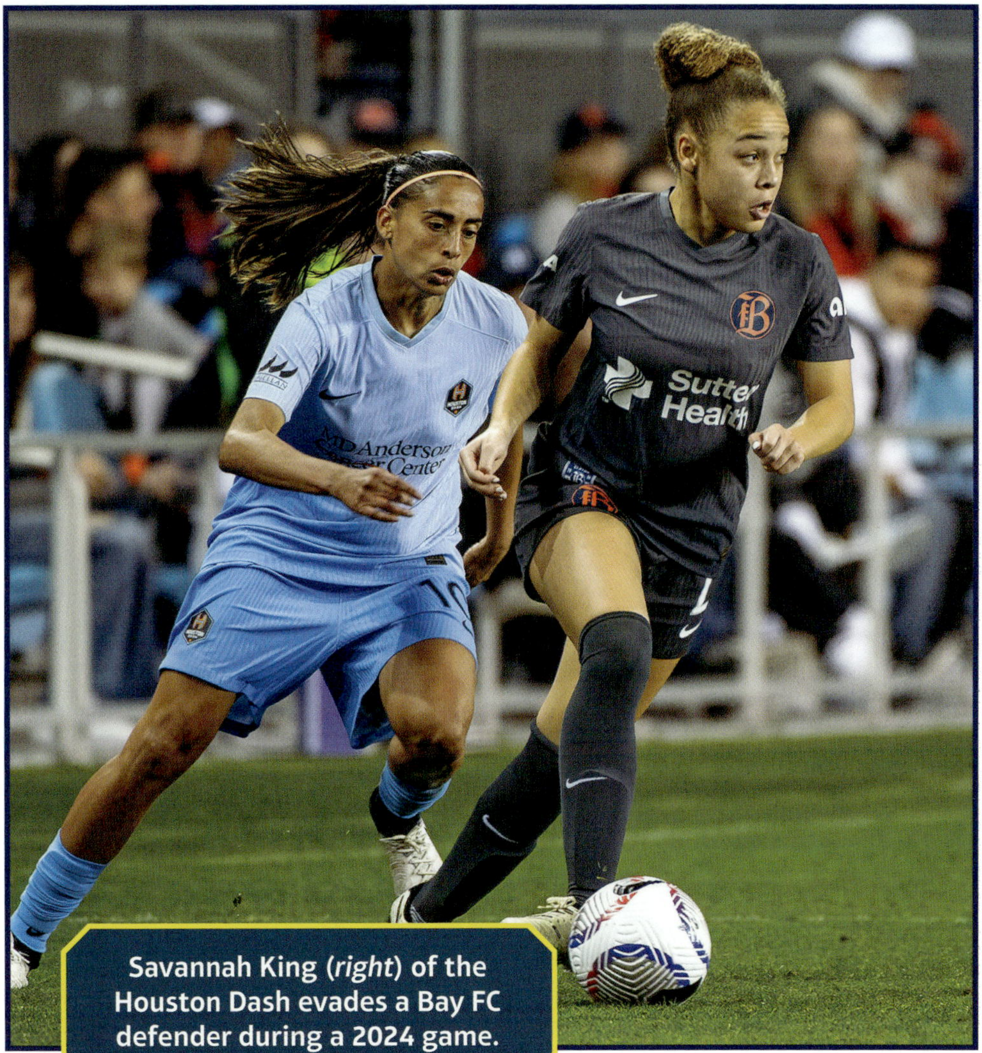

Savannah King (*right*) of the Houston Dash evades a Bay FC defender during a 2024 game.

The league had ups and downs. Some teams didn't sell a lot of tickets or attract many TV viewers. They ran out of money and shut down. But new teams formed and joined the league. In 2024, the NWSL had 14 teams. A team from Boston will join the league in 2026.

Chapter 2

ACTION!

Utah Royals forward Britanny Ratcliffe (*right*) faces a defender in a 2018 game.

The NWSL has given fans many thrilling moments. One came on June 16, 2018, when the Utah Royals took on the powerful North Carolina Courage. The Courage had already won nine games that season without a single loss. They held first place in the league. They seemed unstoppable.

The Royals were a new NWSL team. So far, they had only won 3 of 10 games. People expected the Courage to win big. But for most of the game, neither team could score.

Then, with the game clock winding down, Utah's Brittany Ratcliffe took the ball from a defender and scored. When the final whistle blew, the underdog Royals had won 1–0. The Courage went undefeated the rest of the season and won the league championship. But their one loss to Utah stung.

The North Carolina Courage celebrate after winning the 2018 NWSL championship.

Trinity Rodman of the Washington Spirit dribbles between two Chicago Red Stars defenders.

More excitement came during the 2021 NWSL championship. The Washington Spirit faced the Chicago Red Stars. The Spirit had the fierce rookie Trinity Rodman. She played with fire but couldn't score.

Right before halftime, Chicago's Rachel Hill scored with a header. In the second half, the Spirit tied the game on a penalty kick. The whistle blew with the score stuck at 1–1. The game went to overtime.

Rodman kept up the pressure. Failing to score herself, she passed the ball to Kelley O'Hara, who scored with a header. The Red Stars were hungry to even the score. But Spirit goalkeeper Aubrey Kingsbury blocked shot after shot, holding the Spirit lead. When the whistle blew, the Spirit had won their first NWSL championship.

Kelley O'Hara of the Washington Spirit (*left*) scored with a header during the 2021 NWSL championship.

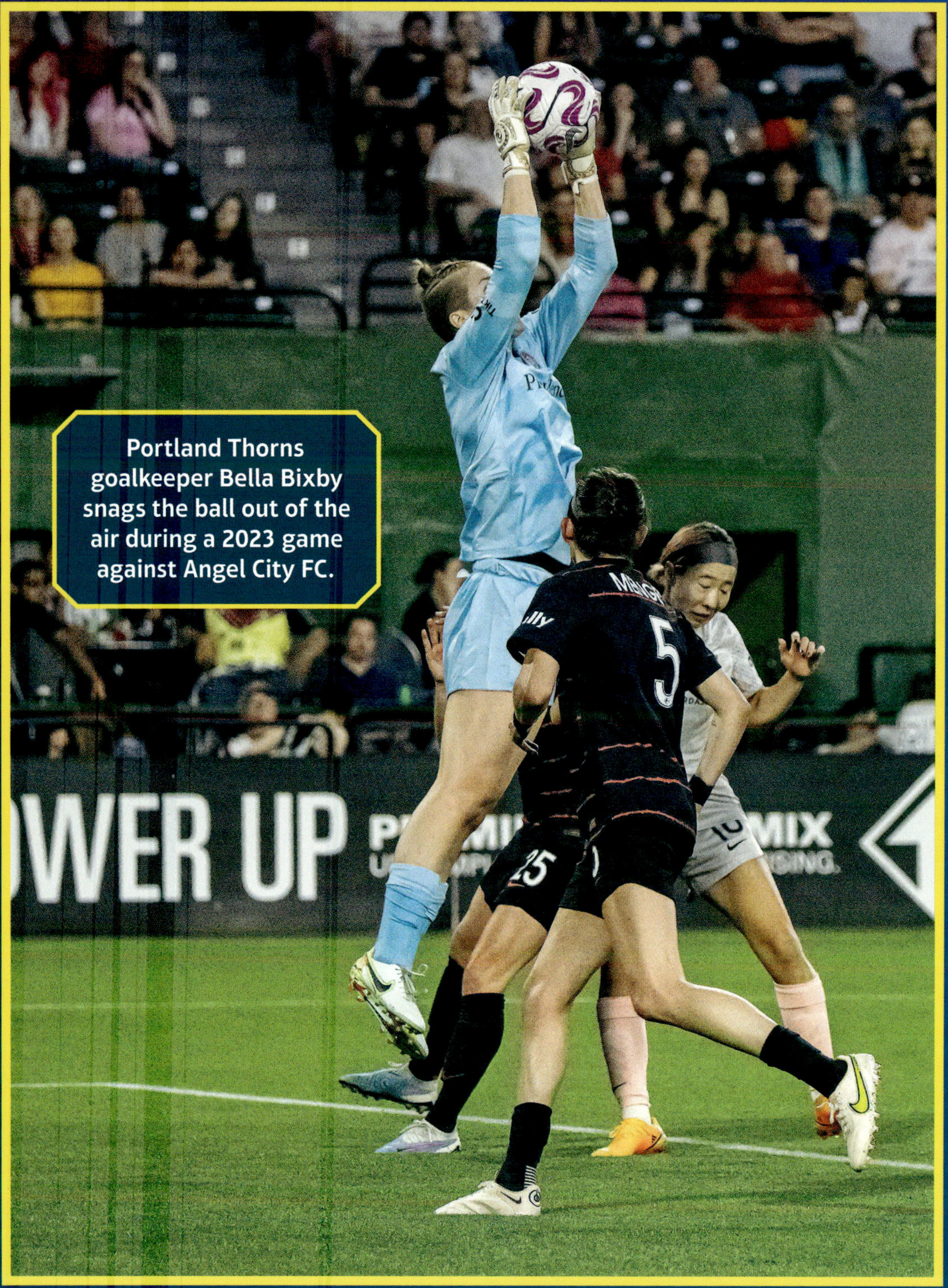

Portland Thorns goalkeeper Bella Bixby snags the ball out of the air during a 2023 game against Angel City FC.

WHAT'S IN A NAME?

Several NWSL teams have the term *football club* (FC) in their name. It comes from Europe. There, soccer is called football. But Americans mostly use the name soccer.

The date was April 29, 2023. It wasn't a championship game, but the 2022 champion Portland Thorns played every game as though a trophy were at stake. In this contest against Angel City FC, Portland was down 3–2 with time running out.

Desperate for a goal, all the Portland players swarmed the Angel City net. Even Portland goalkeeper Bella Bixby

Bella Bixby (*right*) scores the game-winning goal against Angel City FC in 2023.

joined the attack. With players crowding the front of the net, Bixby found the ball and booted it in, saving her team from defeat. It was only the second time in NWSL history that a goalkeeper had scored a goal.

Later that season, on October 15, Angel City and Portland met again. Angel City needed a win to clinch a playoff spot. They did it with an exclamation point. They scored five goals to Portland's one to win the game.

One of those goals came on an incredible bicycle kick by Sydney Leroux. To make this tricky shot, Leroux kicked up one leg and fired the ball backward over her head. Fans around the stadium were shocked when the ball flew past the goalkeeper and into the net.

Sydney Leroux scores with a bicycle kick during a 5–1 victory against Portland.

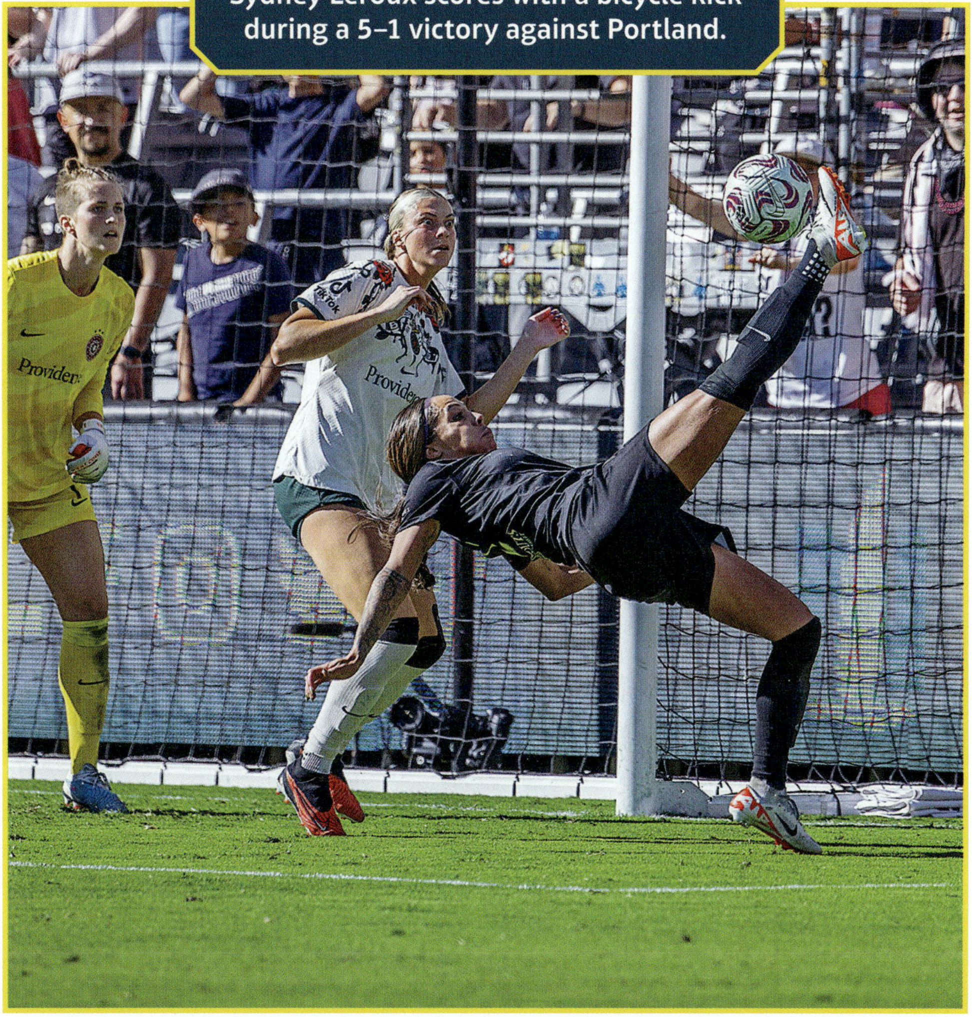

Chapter 3

STAR POWER

Lynn Williams takes a shot during a game against the Orlando Pride in 2020.

The NWSL is loaded with talent. Many of its most famous players are forwards, also called strikers. It's their job to score goals.

Lynn Williams is one of the NWSL's most famous forwards. She joined the league in 2015. She has been raking in honors ever since.

Williams started her pro career on the Western New York Flash. There, she won the 2016 Golden Boot for scoring the most goals that season. She was also named the league's Most Valuable Player (MVP) in 2016. She helped her team win the league championship that year. She won two more championships with the

Lynn Williams shoots the ball during the 2017 NWSL championship game.

North Carolina Courage. She won a fourth with Gotham. Williams has scored more goals than any other player in league history.

Forward Trinity Rodman joined the Washington Spirit in 2021. She made an impact right away. She scored seven goals that year and made seven assists. For this, the NWSL named her Rookie of the Year.

Trinity Rodman races down the field during a 2021 game against the Orlando Pride.

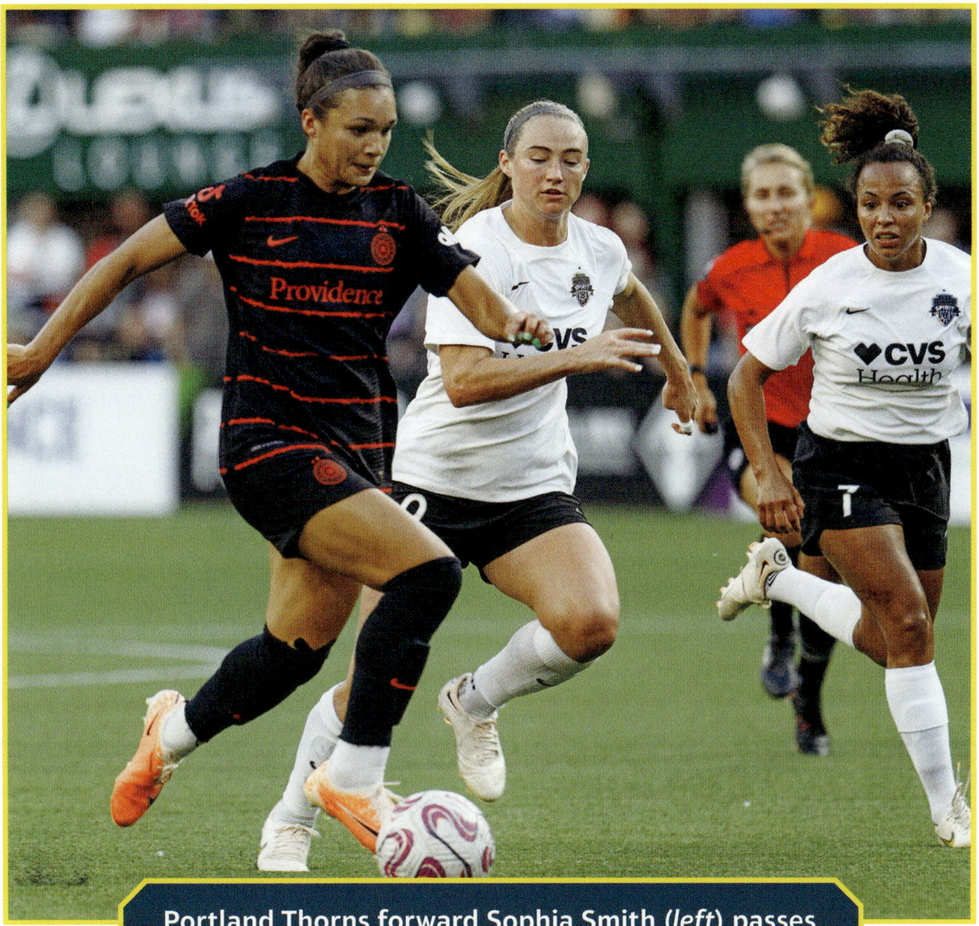

Portland Thorns forward Sophia Smith (*left*) passes two defenders during the 2022 NWSL championship.

A standout at Stanford University, forward Sophia Smith was the first overall pick in the 2020 NWSL draft. She joined the Portland Thorns. It didn't take long for Smith to make her mark on the league. In 2022, she was named league MVP. That year her Thorns won the NWSL championship. The following year, Smith earned the Golden Boot.

Rose Lavelle scores during the 2022 NWSL Challenge Cup.

The NWSL is full of talented midfielders. They play around the centerline of the field. Here, they can play both offense and defense. Famed NWSL midfielders include Savannah DeMelo of Racing Louisville FC, Rose Lavelle of Gotham, and Sam Coffey of the Portland Thorns.

Defenders do the hard work of keeping their opponents from scoring goals. One of the league's top defenders is Naomi Girma. Her position is center back, the heart of the defense. She joined the San Diego Wave in 2022, helping them make the playoffs that year. The league named her Defender of the Year in 2022 and 2023. She was also named Rookie of the Year in 2022.

Naomi Girma (*left*) wrestles the ball away from an attacker during a match between the US and England.

Caprice Dydasco is another powerhouse defender. She began her NWSL career with the Washington Spirit in 2015. She later played for Gotham, the Houston Dash, and Bay FC. While playing for Gotham in 2021, Dydasco was named NWSL Defender of the Year. That year she won more than 60 percent of her tackles, completed almost 80 percent of her passes, and made 49 interceptions.

The last line of defense on a soccer team is the goalkeeper. As balls come flying at the net, she jumps,

Caprice Dydasco (*right*) shoots a header for Bay FC in a 2024 game against Club Amèrica.

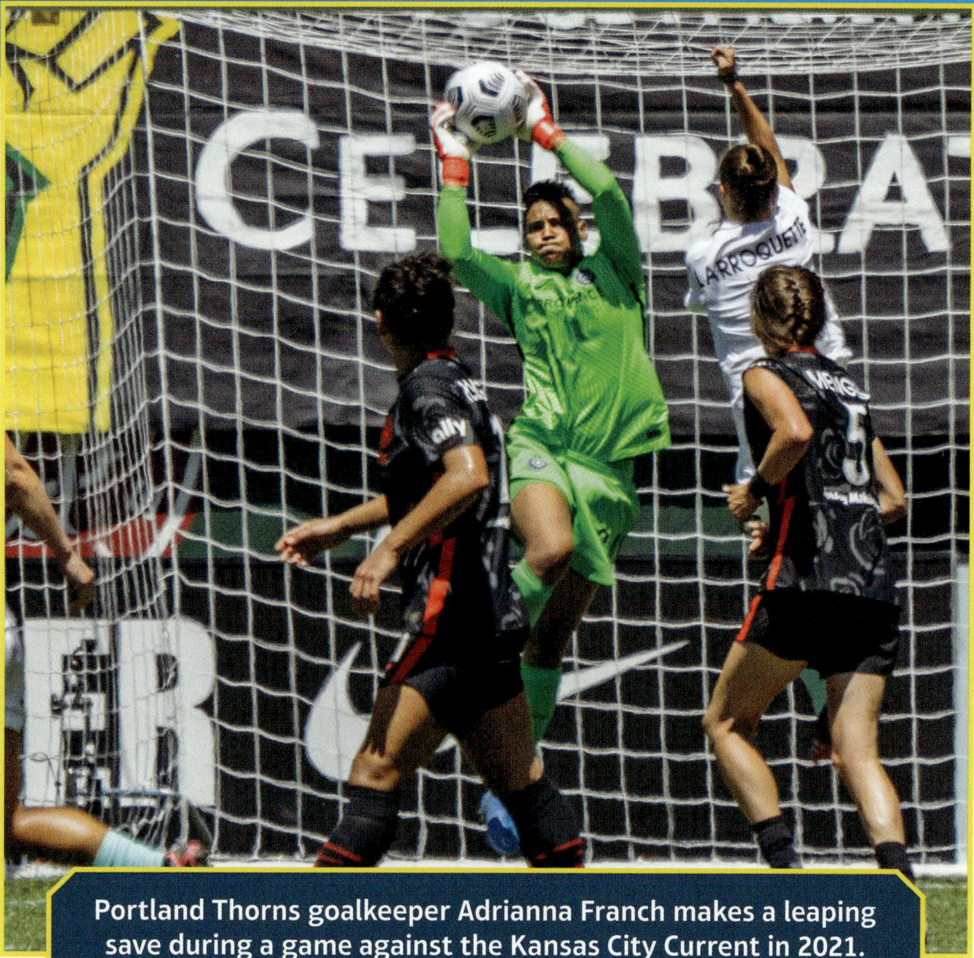

Portland Thorns goalkeeper Adrianna Franch makes a leaping save during a game against the Kansas City Current in 2021.

dives, and slides to deflect them. Adrianna Franch is dynamite at this job. Since joining the NWSL in 2013, she has played for three different teams: the Western New York Flash, the Portland Thorns, and the Kansas City Current.

The year 2017 was huge for Franch. She set the league record for shutouts, was named NWSL Goalkeeper of the Year, and helped her team win the NWSL championship. She was also named Goalkeeper of the Year in 2018.

FOND FAREWELL

Megan Rapinoe is one of the most famous women in soccer. After 10 years, she retired from the NWSL in October 2023. Nearly 700,000 people watched her final game on TV. It was the most watched regular-season game in league history.

Megan Rapinoe waves goodbye to the crowd after her final NWSL game in 2023.

The future of the NWSL looks bright. The league continues to add talented players and form new teams. More people than ever are watching games in person, on TV, and online.

For many years, women's soccer players have been fighting for higher pay. Their paychecks have started to rise and will be higher in the future. The league has also become more diverse, with more women of color playing the sport. No one knows exactly what the future will bring, but one thing is certain: for some of the world's best soccer, fans can count on the NWSL.

Jaedyn Shaw (*right*) of the San Diego Wave tries to avoid a defender during a 2024 match against Gotham.

GLOSSARY

assist: a pass to a teammate that leads directly to a goal

draft: when teams take turns choosing new players

interception: a move that keeps a pass or kick from reaching its target

penalty kick: a free shot at the goal, with only the goalkeeper trying to stop it

playoffs: a series of games played after the regular season to decide the league's champion

professional: taking part in an activity to make money

save: a move by the goalkeeper that keeps the ball out of the net

shutout: a game in which one team never scores a goal

sponsor: a business that gives money to leagues and players in exchange for advertising its products

tackle: using one's feet to take the ball away from an opposing player

World Cup: a big international soccer tournament, played once every four years

LEARN MORE

Girls Soccer Network
https://girlssoccernetwork.com

Goldstein, Margaret. *Meet Sophia Smith*. Minneapolis: Lerner Publications, 2024.

Leed, Percy. *Pro Soccer by the Numbers*. Minneapolis: Lerner Publications, 2025.

McDougall, Chrös. *The Best Women's Players of World Soccer.* Minneapolis: Sportszone, 2024.

National Women's Soccer League
https://www.nwslsoccer.com

Sports Illustrated Kids: Soccer
https://www.sikids.com/tag/soccer

INDEX

PHOTO ACKNOWLEDGMENTS

Image credits: Rich Graessle/Icon Sportswire/Getty Images, p. 4; John Todd/ISI Photos/Getty Images, p. 6; AP Photo/JOHN T. GREILICK, p. 7; Education Images/Universal Images Group/Getty Images, p. 8; Chapman/Mirrorpix/Getty Images, p. 9; AP Photo/Reed Hoffmann, p. 10; Lyndsay Radnedge/ISI Photos/Getty Images, p. 11; Quinn Harris/Icon Sportswire/Getty Images, p. 12; AP Photo/Mark Graves/*The Oregonian*, p. 13; Tim Nwachukwu/Getty Images, p. 14; Tim Nwachukwu/Getty Images, p. 15; Jeff Wong/Sipa USA/Alamy, p. 16; Jeff Wong/Sipa USA/Alamy, p. 18; Ariana Ruiz/ZUMAPRESS/Newscom, p. 19; Brad Smith/ISI Photos/Getty Images, p. 20; Andrew Bershaw/Icon Sportswire/Getty Images, p. 21; Tony Quinn/ISI Photos/Getty Images, p. 22; AP Photo/John Rudoff/Sipa USA, p. 23; AP Photo/Dantey Buitureida/SPP/Sipa USA, p. 24; AP Photo/Kirsty Wigglesworth, p. 25; Eakin Howard/Getty Images, p. 26; AP Photo/Jeff Wong/Sipa USA, p. 27; Steph Chambers/Getty Images, p. 28; AP Photo/Rich Graessle/Icon Sportswire, p. 29.

Design elements: Vect0r0vich/Getty Images; sarayut Thaneerat/Getty Images; sarayut Thaneerat/Getty Images.

Cover: AP Photo/Joe Petro/Icon Sportswire; AP Photo/Dantey Buitureida/SPP/Sipa USA.